RUTH CHOU SIMONS

HARVEST HOUSE PUBLISHERS
EUGENE, OREGON

Unless otherwise indicated, all Scripture quotations are taken from The ESV®
Bible (The Holy Bible, English Standard Version®), copyright © 2001 by Cross-
way, a publishing ministry of Good News Publishers. Used by permission. All
rights reserved.

Cover and interior design by Janelle Coury

Published in association with William K. Jensen Literary Agency, 119 Bampton
Court, Eugene, Oregon 97404.

FIELDS OF JOY

Art and text copyright © 2019 by Ruth Chou Simons
Published by Harvest House Publishers
Eugene, Oregon 97408
www.harvesthousepublishers.com

ISBN 978-0-7369-7217-8

Library of Congress Cataloging-in-Publication Data is on file at the Library of Congress, Washington, DC

Printed in China

20 21 22 23 24 25 26 27 28/ RDS-JC / 10 9 8 7 6 5 4 3 2

Dear friend,

If you're holding this little book in your hands, I'm guessing you and I have an understanding: Joy is sometimes harder to hold onto than it seems. In a world of endless counterfeits, how do we cultivate and experience true joy? How do we "rejoice in the Lord always" (Philippians 4:4)? How do we fight for joy and not give up?

The Word of God draws a bold line between the good news of redemption in Christ and a rejoicing heart. Its pages tell us again and again how we were made for the kind of joy only God can give. If that's true, why, then, do we have to be reminded to rejoice? reminded where joy comes from? reminded of how to respond in trials? The Bible speaks so much of joy and rejoicing because we so easily forget.

These 58 verses and accompanying applications serve as anchors to steady your heart in the fight for joy. We get to preach the truth to our own hearts when we're tempted to trust our eyes or our feelings. I invite you to combat forgetfulness by telling your soul what to do—to rejoice in what is true. I pray these powerful reminders of God's faithfulness drive you to further dependence on His Word and a greater cultivation of lasting joy.

Because of grace,

Ruth

...let the hearts
who seek the Lord
rejoice...

We can always rejoice
when our eyes are fixed on the Lord.

Glory in his holy name;
let the hearts of those who
seek the LORD rejoice!

1 CHRONICLES 16:10

... all rejoice together ...

We were meant to live as one in the
body of Christ, so don't isolate yourself.
Our joy is multiplied when
we rejoice in community.

If one member suffers, all suffer together;
if one member is honored, all rejoice together.

1 CORINTHIANS 12:26

... rejoice
with
truth ...

What we rejoice in will reveal
what we love the most.
When we rejoice in truth,
we show others a love
that is rooted in Christ.

It does not rejoice at wrongdoing, but
rejoices with the truth.

1 CORINTHIANS 13:6

... rejoice with joy
that is
inexpressible ...

What joy awaits us when
we see our Savior face-to-face!
Our future reality shapes our present joy.

Though you have not seen him, you love him.
Though you do not now see him, you believe
in him and rejoice with joy that is inexpressible
and filled with glory, obtaining the outcome
of your faith, the salvation of your souls.

1 PETER 1:8-9

...you may also rejoice
and be glad when
his glory is revealed...

We can rejoice in temporary suffering because our Savior has paid the price for our sin and saved us from eternal suffering.

Rejoice insofar as you share Christ's sufferings, that you may also rejoice and be glad when his glory is revealed.

1 PETER 4:13

... great gain ...

In a world that finds happiness
in earthly treasure,
we find joy in being made more
like Jesus day by day.

Godliness with contentment is great gain...

1 TIMOTHY 6:6

...comfort your hearts and establish them...

Christ is both our eternal and earthly comfort, better than any comfort or joy we could achieve on our own now.

Now may our Lord Jesus Christ himself, and God our Father, who loved us and gave us eternal comfort and good hope through grace, comfort your hearts and establish them in every good work and word.

2 THESSALONIANS 2:16-17

... filled with joy
and with the
Holy Spirit ...

The joy of the Lord cannot flow *from* us
without the Holy Spirit dwelling *in* us.

The disciples were filled with joy
and with the Holy Spirit.

ACTS 13:52

...love, joy, peace...

Joy is a fruit of the Holy Spirit,
assuring us of His work, power,
and presence in our lives.
Just as fruit cannot grow apart
from the vine, joy is formed
only through abiding.

The fruit of the Spirit is love, joy, peace,
patience, kindness, goodness,
faithfulness, gentleness, self-control;
against such things there is no law.

GALATIANS 5:22-23

...I will take joy in the God of my salvation...

The salvation purchased for us
by Christ is
truly our greatest joy.

Yet I will rejoice in the LORD;
I will take joy in the God of my salvation.

HABAKKUK 3:18

... for the joy that was set before him ...

Jesus endured by fixing His eyes
on the joy of God's purpose and plan.
We can run with endurance when
we fix our eyes on Jesus.

Therefore, since we are surrounded by
so great a cloud of witnesses,
let us also lay aside every weight,
and sin which clings so closely,
and let us run with endurance the race
that is set before us, looking to Jesus,
the founder and perfecter of our faith,
who for the joy that was set before him
endured the cross, despising the shame,
and is seated at the right hand of the throne of God.

HEBREWS 12:1-2

...sing for joy, oh heavens...

If you lack joy, recount the ways
God has comforted and cared for you.
Remembering His faithfulness
causes our hearts to
overflow with songs of praise.

Sing for joy, O heavens, and exult, O earth;
break forth, O mountains, into singing!
For the LORD has comforted his people and
will have compassion on his afflicted.

ISAIAH 49:13

...count it all joy...

It may not come naturally,
but by grace we can think of our trials
as joy-inducing because God is using
all things to make us more like Christ.

Count it all joy, my brothers,
when you meet trials of various kinds...

JAMES 1:2

... be glad
and
rejoice ...

We can replace fear with rejoicing
when we remember what God has
already done in our lives.

Fear not, O land; be glad and rejoice,
for the LORD has done great things!

JOEL 2:21

...that my joy
may
be in you...

We were made to be filled up and
satisfied in the joy of the Lord,
made known to us through His Word.

These things I have spoken to you,
that my joy may be in you,
and that your joy may be full.

JOHN 15:11

...that your
joy
may
be full...

God invites us to experience joy as a result of trusting Him as we align our heart's desires with His faithful provision.

Ask, and you will receive, that your joy may be full.

JOHN 16:24

...the presence
of
his glory
with
great joy...

You will know no greater joy
than the assurance that God
preserves and presents you as His.

Now to him who is able to
keep you from stumbling and
to present you blameless
before the presence of his glory
with great joy...

JUDE 24

... good news
of great joy ...

The good news of Christ was utter joy
for those awaiting His arrival and
continues to bring joy to the hearts
of those who realize their need
for a Savior today.

The angel said to them,
"Fear not, for behold,
I bring you good news of great joy
that will be for all the people."

LUKE 2:10

...he delights in steadfast love...

Steadfast love—
something so rare in our experience
that it demands rejoicing when
we experience it in Christ.

Who is a God like you,
pardoning iniquity and passing over
transgression for the remnant of his inheritance?
He does not retain his anger forever,
because he delights in steadfast love.

MICAH 7:18

... rejoice in the Lord always ...

Rejoicing isn't optional or
conditional for believers.
Unlike waves of emotion or excitement,
true joy is unaffected by changes
in circumstances because our hope
in Jesus always remains.

Rejoice in the Lord always;
again I will say, rejoice.

PHILIPPIANS 4:4

...the hope of
the righteous
brings joy...

Sin is deceptive, promising happiness
but never satisfying.
Only pursuing the way of
the Lord leads to lasting joy.

The hope of the righteous brings joy, but the
expectation of the wicked will perish.

PROVERBS 10:28

... a good
word
makes
him glad...

Preaching truth to our own hearts
with the good news of Jesus is
the antidote to anxious thoughts
and our anchor to joy.

Anxiety in a man's heart weighs him down,
but a good word makes him glad.

PROVERBS 12:25

... a joyful
heart is
good medicine ...

What we dwell on in our hearts and minds
carries consequences in our bodies.
The best healing your body can have will
always begin with a heart glad in Him.

A joyful heart is good medicine,
but a crushed spirit dries up the bones.

PROVERBS 17:22

...serve the Lord with gladness...

We can be joyful in our service to the Lord
when we remember our service is
based on relationship, not ritual.
God's presence motivates in a way
duty alone never could.

Serve the LORD with gladness!
Come into his presence with singing!

PSALM 100:2

... it is he
who made us,
we are his ...

It's nearly impossible to be downcast
when we settle it in our hearts once and again
that we belong to our good, good God.

Know that the LORD, he is God!
It is he who made us, and we are his;
we are his people, and the sheep of his pasture.
Enter his gates with thanksgiving,
and his courts with praise!
Give thanks to him; bless his name!

PSALM 100:3-4

...let us rejoice
and be glad...

Each day offers us a choice when it comes
to the joy we will experience and express.
How we approach today is determined
by whom we believe it belongs to.

This is the day that the LORD has made;
let us rejoice and be glad in it.

PSALM 118:24

...your testimonies...
are the joy of my
heart...

God's Word leaves a legacy of joy as
we live by it, build upon it, and let it transform
our minds and shape our hearts.

Your testimonies are my heritage forever,
for they are the joy of my heart.

PSALM 119:111

...your promise
gives me
life...

Even in pain and difficulty,
we can turn to the truths of God's Word,
which promise to comfort and sustain.

This is my comfort in my affliction,
that your promise gives me life.

PSALM 119:50

... we are glad ...

We will not lack gladness
if we are perpetually recounting
the good and merciful works
of the Lord in our lives.

The LORD has done great things for us;
we are glad.

PSALM 126:3

...shall reap with shouts of joy...

Tears will not last forever!
There is a day coming when
God will wipe away every tear and
joy will be our constant reality.

Those who sow in tears
shall reap with shouts of joy!

PSALM 126:5

...my heart shall rejoice in your salvation...

Where do you put your trust?
If it's in God's unchanging, unyielding love,
you can be assured that His rescue
and salvation are secure as well.

I have trusted in your steadfast love;
my heart shall rejoice in your salvation.

PSALM 13:5

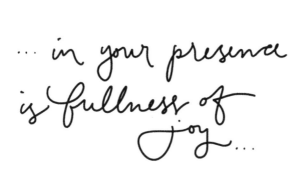

... in your presence
is fullness of
joy ...

We were created to know fullness of joy
by nearness to God as He leads, directs,
and satisfies us with His presence.

You make known to me the path of life;
in your presence there is fullness of joy;
at your right hand are pleasures forevermore.

PSALM 16:11

...he delighted in me...

Let this fill you with joy as it humbles your heart:
We have been rescued because
the God of the universe delighted in us—
not by any merit of our own but simply
because He purposed to rescue us.

He brought me out into a broad place;
he rescued me, because he delighted in me.

PSALM 18:19

...rejoicing
the heart...

Combat indifference and weariness with biblical truth. It brings joy, hope, and light to the heart that receives it.

...the precepts of the LORD are right, rejoicing the heart; the commandment of the LORD is pure, enlightening the eyes...

PSALM 19:8

... rejoice with
Trembling ...

Our joy is built on a holy reverence for an awesome (in the truest sense of the word) God. The more we are in awe of Him, the less we will try to find our joy in counterfeits.

Serve the LORD with fear,
and rejoice with trembling.

PSALM 2:11

...glad with
the joy of
your
presence...

When God gives us His presence,
He promises the blessing of never again
being alone or dependent on only ourselves.

You make him most blessed forever;
you make him glad with
the joy of your presence.

PSALM 21:6

... they comfort me ...

Even when our circumstances appear grim,
we have the comfort and safety of
our Good Shepherd who goes with us,
even through the darkest valleys.

Even though I walk through the valley
of the shadow of death,
I will fear no evil, for you are with me;
your rod and your staff, they comfort me.

PSALM 23:4

...joy comes
with
the morning...

Maybe you're in a night season...
remember that morning is coming.
Whether it's here or in eternity with Christ,
joy will prevail even as the cross
overcame the grave.

His anger is but for a moment,
and his favor is for a lifetime.
Weeping may tarry for the night,
but joy comes with the morning.

PSALM 30:5

... I will rejoice
and be glad in
your steadfast love...

When we stop and remember God's omniscience
(that He sees us and knows us),
we find joy in His faithfulness, knowing that
nothing escapes His care and wisdom.

I will rejoice and be glad in your steadfast love,
because you have seen my affliction;
you have known the distress of my soul...

PSALM 31:7

...Shout for joy,
all you upright
in heart...

Replace wallowing in despair over your sin
with rejoicing over your forgiveness in Christ.
When we receive His righteousness as
our own, we can finally know true joy.

Be glad in the LORD, and rejoice, O righteous,
and shout for joy, all you upright in heart!

PSALM 32:11

... our heart is glad in him ...

Trust begets joy when anchored to
a Savior whose purposes are
always His glory and our good.

Our heart is glad in him,
because we trust in his holy name.

PSALM 33:21

...the abundance
of your house...

God's resources abundantly provide —
in more ways than temporary
fixes or momentary satisfaction.
He fills us up with His bounty of grace.

They feast on the abundance of your house,
and you give them drink from the river of your delights.

PSALM 36:8

...may all
who seek you
rejoice...

Good news: You will never be saved
by your own greatness.
God is great and mighty enough to save...
enough to be all that you need.

But may all who seek you
rejoice and be glad in you;
may those who love your salvation say
continually, "Great is the LORD!"

PSALM 40:16

...let the
bones
that you
have
broken
rejoice...

Nothing heals, restores, and brings joy
like the good news of Christ—that in Him
our deepest pain, our brokenness,
and the power of sin is made no more.
Hard-to-heal spaces don't merely
find temporary relief in Jesus—
they are made new and rejoice.

Purge me with hyssop, and I shall be clean;
wash me, and I shall be whiter than snow.
Let me hear joy and gladness;
let the bones that you have broken rejoice.

PSALM 51:7-8

... the hills
gird themselves
with
joy ...

The earth testifies to God's faithfulness.
Look up from your circumstances and
see how they praise their creator.
If creation declares His greatness in
the most ordinary ways, so should we.

The pastures of the wilderness overflow,
the hills gird themselves with joy, the meadows clothe
themselves with flocks, the valleys deck themselves
with grain, they shout and sing together for joy.

PSALM 65:12-13

...let the nations
be glad and
sing for joy...

We don't place our hope in kingdoms, nations, or rulers. We trust in the God who holds all things together.

Let the nations be glad and sing for joy, for you judge the peoples with equity and guide the nations upon earth. *Selah*

PSALM 67:4

... my lips will
shout for joy ...

Jesus doesn't offer us merely
a good day or a happy circumstance.
He redeems the soul.

.

My lips will shout for joy,
when I sing praises to you;
my soul also, which you have redeemed.

PSALM 71:23

...my heart and flesh sing for joy...

That longing you feel?
It won't find rest anywhere
but in God's presence. There is no shelter
like our dwelling place with Him.

My soul longs, yes, faints for the courts of the LORD;
my heart and flesh sing for joy to the living God.

PSALM 84:2

...that ye may rejoice and be glad...

We were made to be satisfied
and glad in Christ.
No simple solution, clean house,
job promotion, or dream realized
will ever satisfy like God's unfailing love.

Satisfy us in the morning
with your steadfast love,
that we may rejoice and
be glad all our days.

PSALM 90:14

...at the works of
your hands
I sing for joy...

Recount the work of the Lord in your life,
and you will find yourself rehearsing
the truth of His lovingkindness.

You, O LORD, have made me glad by your work;
at the works of your hands I sing for joy.

PSALM 92:4

... let us
make a
joyful
noise ...

We were made for worship, for praise,
for awe in His presence.
God has put a song in our hearts
that cannot be sung apart from
response to Him.

Oh come, let us sing to the LORD;
let us make a joyful noise to the rock of our salvation!
Let us come into his presence with thanksgiving;
let us make a joyful noise to him
with songs of praise!

PSALM 95:1-2

... rejoice in the Lord ...

"None is righteous, no, not one"
(Romans 3:10) is the painful truth,
but God's holiness in our place is the good news...
one worthy of rejoicing in today.

Rejoice in the LORD, O you righteous,
and give thanks to his holy name!

PSALM 97:12

...make a joyful noise
to the Lord...

Let's take seriously the instruction to sing,
to declare, and to praise.
The heart that is rescued in Christ is the heart
that overflows with uncontained praise.

Make a joyful noise to the LORD,
all the earth; break forth into
joyous song and sing praises!

PSALM 98:4

... rejoice in hope...

When we cultivate rejoicing,
patience, and perseverance in prayer,
we experience the transforming
work of the gospel in our lives.

Rejoice in hope,
be patient in tribulation,
be constant in prayer.

ROMANS 12:12

...righteousness
and peace and
joy in
the Holy Spirit...

Don't settle for lesser things.
God has created you to be filled up
with what only the Spirit can
supply and sustain.

The kingdom of God is not a matter of
eating and drinking but of righteousness
and peace and joy in the Holy Spirit.

ROMANS 14:17

...fill you with
all joy and
peace
in believing...

Hope fuels and fans the flames
of joy and peace.

May the God of hope fill you with all joy and
peace in believing, so that by the power of
the Holy Spirit you may abound in hope.

ROMANS 15:13

... we rejoice
in the hope
of the
glory of God...

Only a child of God knows that the Lord transforms our sufferings into hope, and only a child of God is crazy enough to rejoice in them. The grace of God makes impossible joy possible.

Through him we have also obtained access by faith into this grace in which we stand, and we rejoice in hope of the glory of God. Not only that, but we rejoice in our sufferings, knowing that suffering produces endurance, and endurance produces character, and character produces hope, and hope does not put us to shame, because God's love has been poured into our hearts through the Holy Spirit who has been given to us.

ROMANS 5:2-5

God's love for us isn't rooted in
our loveliness or worthiness, but in His own.
He chooses to save us—right in the midst of
our mess—and win our hearts over
with His extravagant love.

The LORD your God is in your midst,
a mighty one who will save; he will rejoice
over you with gladness; he will quiet you by his love;
he will exult over you with loud singing.

ZEPHANIAH 3:17

RUTH CHOU SIMONS

is a bestselling author, entrepreneur, and speaker. She shares her journey of God's grace intersecting daily life with word and paintbrush through an online shoppe at **GraceLaced.com** and her Instagram community of more than a hundred thousand. Ruth and her husband, Troy, are grateful parents to six boys— their greatest adventure. Ruth's first book, *GraceLaced*, won a 2018 Christian Book Award.